I Believe I Was The Moon

By Spirit-C

ISBN: 9798401612793

1. INTRODUCTION LETTER

<u>TRUE POETRY (PART ONE)</u>

Try to <u>understand</u> me. Pain in my veins, I can barely sleep. I look to the skies as I wonder why. **Where does the actual truth lie?** I'm like a bird that can't fly. <u>Hoping</u> one of these days, he can touch the sky. **Have wings <u>but</u> can't go high.**

Should clip the wings, so his dreams she'll lie. But he **rose like a lion** with <u>no clan</u>. But as soon as he finds his kin, he soon realizes that he is the <u>better</u> Man. Within his Kin, they take notice and <u>Crown</u> him for all **who truly understand.** Like all great Men, <u>some</u> **rejected him. Sowing Seeds** of <u>Thorns</u> for all who truly understand.

Some seeds got <u>uprooted</u> as time got saved in their hands. While others let the Seeds sprout, **in return allowing the Seeds of Thorns to be deeply rooted within.** <u>Hard</u> to **tow out, even after seeing the Err within.** They try to change their minds but <u>resort back</u> **lounged in the Thorn-Vines that the mind is still Trapped in. Be patient. It takes time for you to flee the Web you created inside.** You will end up <u>cut,</u> probably even have **Thorns stuck within.**

But as the time comes, your wounds <u>will</u> heal inside. **Look to the skies, find the signs. Do Right and Forgive, and a blessing will come in time.**

~SC

2. FOR YOU

<u>Granny Love...</u>

I write this to you with tears in my pen.

You were there to comfort me.

You were there to help discover me.

Now I'm uncovered.

Now I'm growing thinking of God.

Without you,

it would have been different.

Just filled with a living spirit.

That doesn't have a mission.

I know God's plan for you is tremendous.

Just like now,

lavished plans are here for you in your earthly home.

Without you, I would be completely alone.

But I'm secure because you'll be home.

You make me know I'll never be alone. ~SC

<u>3. YOUTH</u>

<u>Blood Pen</u>

Pen inside this Blood.
Blood within this Pen.
I write and write, bleeding from the inside. Spirit CRY, looking for my SUNSHINE. But at last, it's only moonlight. How long will it take to realize?
My pen bleeds.
Yes, it cries.
Narrated stories of typical lives. Just see, WAIT, you'll see! "Every Poem tells a life." Wheel of Fortune NO! My Fortune is a bright light.
Bright,
as,
can,
be,
like a lighthouse, I'll guide. Ink black and Blue that in my veins, that in my mind. You are a gift, your life. With my pen blood, I'll be alright.
~SC

<u>**Life Choices**</u>

Analyzing two crossroads of my mind.
What I perceive is one to be more solvent than the other.
I'm like the trunk of a tree.
The limbs stretch out where the arms can be.
One of the limbs likes to deceive.
It's Always trying to have me pay a fee.
Can somebody reach to take the lead?
Still is institutionalized by what I perceive.
Another individual would have called it a street of a dream.
Running from the lock, it doesn't include me!
Analyzing two crossroads of my mind.
~SC

<u>**Don't Know**</u>

I'm sitting here trying to keep the peace.
Step on my toes, still attempting to trip me.
I'm just not knowing.
I'm still trying not to react to everything.
I'm keeping myself calm. That is the best response to be.
But at last, I know me.
I need to change the outcome of my life for me.
Because if I don't, then where will I be?

Now fool, what even makes you think you even know
me.
I called you a fool because it's so clear to see.
You don't even know what this face I show means.
~SC

<u>Seeing</u>

You see, yet you are very much still blind.
Blinded by the enemies of the mind. Look outside of
the mind. Think with your eyes. See what you can find?
Not yet wait it's still coming in due time. ~SC

<u>4. Detached</u>

<u>**Phases**</u>

I believed I was the **moon**.
The modification of **waves** while I **swing**.
The night brings out different **Phases** of me.
Some I never knew to belong to me.
The worst phases **persuade** the tides.
Colliding accordingly to the stones,
that it is **forced** to feed.
As **divine** as that sounds,
it's truthfully **wicked** within.
Inspire and **per sway**, as you can.
My phases are here, and they stay to **prevail**.
I believed I was the **moon**.
With different faces playing **pretend**.
But I know when a full moon emerges,
These tides **won't** stand. ~SC

<u>**Spoke**</u>

Look and listen to the words I got to say.
For this not to be for the modern-day.
I speak of a past, of a troubled mind misunderstood,
by emotions that are hard to be declined.
So, in the light, he reached out his arm blessed with the
understanding gift at a young age.
For so young they questioned why he was so wise?
He talked, but people didn't comprehend the words he
spoke.

Stop preaching, silenced off they did.
For his age, he was just a kid.
Taking in every element of his life.
soon became what he spoke was life.
~SC

<u>Black Sheep</u>

"When Guilt Starts Understand Cause Guilt Can Strike"

Been <u>W</u>orried,

been <u>G</u>ifted,

been <u>S</u>tressed,

been hated by many of humankind.
The ones I know that have been on my mind.
You said you, love,
I'm noticing hate.
You said you, love,
I'm noticing fake love every day.
Drill gaps in my mind.
Unknowing planting seeds of,

<u>U</u>nlove,

<u>C</u>ontempt,

and <u>G</u>uilt.

Some I think about thought out the days.
Thinking my problems aren't that great.
You see what You see.
Not what I embrace.
People's destiny doesn't see them apart.

<u>C</u>ry

or

<u>S</u>ad

dust it off your shoulders like sand from an hourglass.
~SC

<u>I'll fly</u>

This is me. This is who I'll she'll be.

I take a breath of life while I speak. Fill me up I need it give it to me.

Do you believe a single word can fill you up where you can be as satisfied as can be? Take your time you will see what it be. You lust something that spark that battery. Try love to be your peace. Invite it in. Let it sleep.

It been gone to long for it to be out in the streets.

Love is all we truly need. Truth be told I'll probably just saying this to me.

But I know one thing. I starting to feel healthier then was to be.

 No anger, no depression will loosen me. Keep my happiness in order and let's see where it'll lead.

And no.

I'm not sitting here just trying to preach. I'm really telling you that I need the truth to be able to see. Maybe mainly talking to me. But I know in my time, in no time I'll be lifted off my feet.

I'll fly, I'll fly, I'll fly

I hope heaven can speak.

~SC

<u>DARK</u>

In the dark dawn a star
Leading in the dark
Blaze from afar
Little car, but big heart leading big cars
Kirby star, heart beating hard
Gavin up, but got a jump star
Not fame, but respect drawn up hard. ~SC

5. Cupid Love

<u>Loving</u>

Loving someone can sometimes hurt. I put my faith in love so I can hope to fide the peace I need from this pain that hurts. Been marinating in a mid-deep cold breeze from the sea of a Stormy mist that is clouding me. But at last, I came close to a light that I see as a lighthouse that give a bright light from the stormy mist that clouded me from afar. I'm seeing light from the storm and hope is not so far still got tides but they dying down cause the island is in our heart. I really believe that this trip I have come so far out on the sea now I'm starting a trip to see what on this island I have loving came on.

She was giving me a good start, giving me a good heart. But still haven't left the dock. I look in her eye I just see a shooting star. You look in her eye you see a black space that separate you apart. I hold her I can stop feeling a love in her heart. I kiss her I think about it a lot. I hold her in, and it's like I'm the one in her arms. She a home to a falling star.

Love Struck

Love.
    Love.
It's like a dove.
    Love.
  Love.
It's like a dove as pure as good.
Love would bring what it should.
Love is the key we need.
For us all to be at heavenly peace.
At peace is the key to the life we desperately need.
When you love powerful, it is like a mountain now sing along.
When your hurt by love, it's like cupid missed his target.
So, he pulls the arrow out to shoot it where it belongs.
Like the love of a newborn baby, the hearts connected.
Strings are tied strong.
But love, where do I belong?
What can I call home?
From the birds who have a nest also called "a home."
From the bees, that so many do what the queen longs.
Should I move faster than a plane in the sky?
Or should I move slower than a slug?
Ten mins went by it's still on my porch carrying along.
Love is not a word.
Love it's not only a verb.
Love is a life path that we all see AND WANT IT TO

BELONG.
~SC

<u>WaterWorks</u>

Dear Love, why is the rain coming so hard? I had yet to get wet while I waited for you from afar. You left. Where are you? Feed me some love. My love, starting to starve. How long will I make it? My heart is driving on E. You were my last stop. Rain is coming down so hard. I started to get drenched all over, including the holes where my eyes are.

Sincerely, SC

<u>Respect</u>

I respect you.
I respect him.
I respect her.
Where is the respect for me? I've been nice. I give, I decline
to receive.
So, were you when I truly needed it? Sometimes I lock the
key to the heart. But your lock opened but yet they paid
free of charge. Truth be told, I cannot forget I did push
start. I guess I am in custody of this low respect to my
heart ~SC

Love Or Lust

You have hurt me to the point I don't know what is what. Your love is more than love, it's' lust. And if I lust, will it be strong enough then it must? But babe, listen. Why are you always saying the questionable but? Telling me this, then you tell me that. The words you speak are like poison at its touch. This is the life of another relationship, blowing in the dust. Her touch is so soft, feel it on the hairs of the arm as she brush.
Sweet messages telling me she wants love. Should I lay down and let her control the clutch? I might have just hopped up and got on better stuff.
But forget all that I'm tied by a string, being pulled in the dark. Been on this freeway so long I should have been charged.
Your love is more than love it's' lust. ~SC

<u>6. Mind-Power(poem)</u>

MIND-POWER

All this time I have been trying to fix my mind.
But no one sees how much I have been trying.
They think I am the same hollow person inside with half a mind.
They just don't know inside; I have a blossom one in a kind mind
Unique as a rare dime.
If I push, I will prosper within time.
No one understands my mind.
So, they treat me like a 01-penny touch by every line.
But for me, oh me I've seen the mask you can't hide the lie.
You read this, but you will never understand my mind.
But within my time I know I will fly.
How high?
I don't know, I just have faith within the inside.
I will fly
I WILL FLY!
But if I fly and look down.
Will I be like a comet in the sky?
Coming down so fast, so hard.
About time it connects with the skin of the ball of life on the outside.
I will be like a fly who just needs to try to fly.
But I found help from the one who owns the sky.
He told me, son, just fly.
I thank the owner of the sky.
He is the owner of everything including my mind.
But like a jet, he shot the bad bugs out the sky.

I know I still have favor in his eyes.
But back to what I was saying this is really a plane over your mind.
I hope now you see how complex is the mind.
~SC

7. Chocolate Love

<u>Sugar Rush</u>

My dark Coco <u>Sista</u>
and <u>Brotha</u>.
Do you not see?
That beauty in your skin is as sweet as can be.
The brown sugar gets sticky when it's wet.
So why can't <u>we</u>?
My <u>Sista</u>.
My <u>Brotha</u>.
And let us not forget about the,
Honey and Caramel.
That holds a sweet taste when <u>We</u> feed.
<u>We</u> are all sweet.
Same, but a different breed.
Smile with the beauty we hold within <u>We</u>.
I smile.
You smile.
We see the beauty within <u>We</u>.
And I can't deny that I need.
I need a society where all the sugary sweets.
Can just melt and breathe.
White sugar only got one breed.
But still sweet.
So, arrive to melt with <u>we</u>.
Melt away the worries.
Melt away the pain.
Melt away the crimes we hide in our brains.
And now imagine how sweet that will
be..., to <u>You</u>..., to <u>We</u>. ~SC

<u>Blind</u>

All this time.
We have been endowed by the one in a kind.
That we eyed as the divine.
We praise Blind.
But have faith that we are safe in his eyes.
We try to be satisfied.
But must fail every try.
Why must there be a why?
Sin is an everyday try.
Escape?
I like to see you try.
There is no need to explain why.
We live.
We die.
Just to do it right.
Time is a story that we write every life.
Give to a life we made to give them a try.
When we are gone, will they have to gain?
Just to live their desired life.
The stuff you learned to do.
Not to do.
And the exact reasons why.
Just won't be the same in their eye of the mind.
You can try to tell.

You can try to teach.
But it'll be water down by the lack of knowledge.
Raised in their youthful mind.
The youth are growing to understand.
A period where violence is the trend.
Satisfied with life within my skin of culture.
We can't deny it.
We chose not to believe nor have the time.
To bring it up without a try.
But it's still vivid in the eye.
We praise the areas that we chose to remain.
Yet it's hard to maintain.
We pick to it and make it our culture.
That worldly people selected to envision us in their brain.
I'm not BLACK.
I would say not a Nigga.
But still, use it in everyday slag.
I'm African, Blacker than the sky.
Golden Brown That fits me well.
I love my Golden-Brown compilation.
I know I was gifted by the divine to mold from the clay.
Just to try to live with it well.
~SC

<u>**Who Matters**</u>

Truth be told didn't have a lot.
But I had a lot.
Didn't know my soul was touched.
By the smooth sweet hands of my grandma, I love so
much.
But there was lust.
Lust of a fuss of a group that grew up tough.
Shortly later the lust turned into love.
What stereotypes would gratefully and relentlessly label as
thugs.
Institutionalized in the mindset and the eyes of me.
I had locked on to the contacts in me, the friends to me.
Once in a full moon of my reality, they would sense the
sweet love that was still in me.
They questioned and tried to clown me.
To put me back in sync with the hidden life of me.
I forced my way to be seen as what I wanted to be.
But it turned that into me.
Emotions sore rain poured in while all the sessions
changed.
Just to learn more.
Never found a door to leave.
So, this reality I gratefully and cautiously explore.
Times got rough.
I just had to endure.
My soul WAS...IS, trapped in chains of a shaken fool who

had an opportunity to change for more.
I have seen people on the news.
Some even grew to hear of or knew.
Real story?

Who knows?
We scream free who matters in my city.
But they only matter to you.
Please let us stop playing the trending topic fool.
~SC

8. Revolution (REV)

<u>Looming</u>

Looming in a room waiting for an answer.
For a blessing because u had mistaken life.
I have mistaken life to be a different breed of a lesson.
blessed to the one that I had hurt.
I'm supposed to learn then give it back.
Removing the thorns.
I'm looming for a future of whom I'll be.
I'm breathing so there life in me.
I breathe cause life is inviting me.
Looming on a 2nd floor window.
Looking out the window viewing life from the within.
Still feeling like I'm on the outside in.
I'm looming to peek a new horizon.
Hopefully I seen be riding in.
A new horizon if it given will I win?
Looming walking down the street,
still while there people looking at me.
They don't ask, but I know they asking me.
Who am I that I be?
Different people just not me.
Leave me alone.
Let my spirit be. ~SC

<u>**Tired**</u>
I'm tired.
Weak.
But still can't sleep
I weep, but it seems I'm still weak.
God was by my side but waiting on me.
I still have the same thoughts that could injure me.
When will I sleep?
It's late in the night when I do sleep.
I dream.
Good or Bad, occasionally the message is not vivid to me.
So tired, but there are still stories to teach.
~SC

<u>**OWE**</u>

A high power is the name that I know.
Within him, I grow.
One day I'll prosper from the one I know.
I must learn to respect before I go
With you, my King my love will show.
My mind, my power will grow and prosper
FOREVERMORE.
I'm a King in a kingdom with lions at my door.
Alpha lion but serve the Lord.
So much Mind-Power it's crazy what all I know.
Trust that I know I reap what I sow.
When the kingdom comes.
Oh, I know.

I'm in the love of the Lord.
But I must give back what I owe.
And I owe love, respect, and so-much mo.
~SC

<u>TEMPLE</u>

<u>*Wisdom is key.*</u>
<u>*Lay a brick.*</u>
<u>*What will it be?*</u>
<u>*How many bricks will it take to build the wall you wish to see.*</u>
<u>*Will you gain prosperity?*</u>
<u>*Or will you make a wall where the river seems to be?*</u>
<u>*A mental growth is needing to put my spirit where my flesh be.*</u>
<u>*Understand I'm Spirit-C.*</u>
<u>*No this is no conspiracy.*</u>
<u>*Do you see your reality?*</u>
<u>*I see mine and I'll prosper down to my feet.*</u>
<u>*Might as well call me happy feet, but the wisdom of a youth king.*</u>
<u>*Wisdom is power.*</u>
<u>*I'm not even in my final hour.*</u>
<u>*Mind delicate as a flower.*</u>
<u>*So small but holds so much beautiful power.*</u>
<u>*All you need is a muster seed of faith.*</u>
<u>*You'll see what it'll bring.*</u>
<u>*We lay brinks every day.*</u>
<u>*but what are we truly making?*</u>
<u>*~SC*</u>

Peace?

For the world this is what I wrote.
peace to the world that it she'll never be hold.
For the world's humbleness, it should behold.
Just trying to be keeping us at hold.
for us we don't know what is hold.
want peace, but don't know where it fell in a hole.
who she'll be the one to bring us and put the sinner growth
to the hold.
for we just mortal people with no time to hold.
Stuff I don't know but want the peace that like a mother
kangaroo its joey it will hold.
Peace like a river it will flow, but not too strong it waters it
can't hold.
~SC

9. HELLO!

<u>PERRY</u>

Let me inspire the.
The mind where your knowledge be.
Do you think you can get the best of me?
But for me, I'm smarter than most think.
Y'all think I'm a Perry.
But undercover me Perry got secrets.
Secrets that will be a mystery to the way you think.
Mysteries go ahead and call me.
Cause of me this is just another poem riding on the mind
of the. ~SC

<u>The jig is up!</u>

Hey there! Why do you be a lie? You got a hollow lie. You
were a friend, but around crowds, you put up different
masks of lies.
Hoping I lie with you?
THE JIG IS UP!
I see the inside. But who am I? Sometimes I also wear a
mask to block the black eye.
THE JIG IS UP!
I need to show my eye. Saw real life. Real-life slap my eye.
THE JIG IS UP!
Life doesn't lie. Parents tell kids a fat man is coming inside.
We need to celebrate Jesus, the man who saved our lives.
THE JIG IS UP!!
most likely we know we just give our kids a smiling lie.
~SC

<u>PHONES</u>

Hello?
Are you there?
I have been calling you for the last hour I know you're aware.
Hello?
Why declines my call?
I know you sit there and stair.
BABE!
Were you aware?
I know you are still in your co-worker's lair. It hurt so much knowing you don't care. I even found his underwear...
~SC

<u>The Looker</u>

From the corner of the edge of my eye, I feel you.
You looking!
Is it cause I'm cute?
IS it because I did a crime I never knew?
The answer is deep in you.

VERMIN

You fool, you thought I wouldn't see you?
YES, YOU!
Over there with that suspicious attitude.
You thought you got away from me?
Maybe you thought I wouldn't, see?
NAH!
I have been watching the hole where you sleep.
I set traps hoping you take the cheese.
But shoot!
YOU ARE SMARTER THAN ME!
You dang vermin, why won't you stay asleep?
You the mouse, I'm the person who cants help but sees.
Can someone take care of this mouse for me?
~SC

10. OUTRO

<u>TRUE POETRY (PART TWO)</u>

There is a <u>higher power</u> when is it will you realize?
As humans, we sin **all the time.**
As a <u>sinner,</u> **is it better to not know than to know?**
If you sin and if you know, **how much does that**
weighted value truthfully hold?
But there is <u>no</u> one man perfect just to let you know.
We all sin, sometimes we don't even know.
But just know the <u>Higher</u>, **he knows.**
People <u>come</u> and <u>go</u>.
Timing it just <u>never</u> holds.
Just to let you know I **<u>speak</u> what I know.**
And if I'm wrong, please correct what I know.
But with that being told, show <u>proof</u> so I can be exposed.
But if you can't show your evidence, I guess I will never
know.
While truth be told in time I'll probably know.
If God allows me in the spot, so I can be exposed.
If Lord do then the <u>timing</u> **was right for me to know.**
Might be <u>days</u>, <u>weeks</u>, <u>months</u>, or <u>years</u>.
But **God's timing is always right.**
There was a time where I was trying to understand.
But the timing wasn't right.
I was just an <u>infant</u> to the **living knowledge.**
But as time flew, I grew.
Only a few can know how deeply it had to grew.
But never knew what **thinking process was intervening.**
Making what **I said and show just won't even come**
close to being seen.

Where is it we must go?
The place we call but I call is the <u>after home.</u>
Is it filled with the **riches that we value as <u>diamonds</u> and <u>pearls</u>?**
It is an <u>untold</u> story that will **be given, in our due time?**
Our bodies are filled with <u>water</u> and <u>sand</u> that is given a "<u>soul</u>" to give us "<u>life</u>".
So, with all this being said, I have a question for your mind.
What is the <u>value</u> of your <u>life</u>?
Where do your <u>soul</u> and <u>spirit</u> call <u>home</u> until you can't open your eyes?
~SC

<u>*SINCERELY, SPIRIT-C AKA SC*</u>

ABOUT THE AUTHOR

My name is Clinton Williams but go by C.J. or my poetic name SC. I was born on Aug 27, 2001, and I was risen, in Dallas, TX. This book tells a life, that was brought to me by me. This story was given to me as a youthful African American male. I was blindsided by traps that I was given to myself formed by myself. I made this to breathe life in people, every poem tells a life. Every poem breathes and is alive. Read them with the energy that was meant to belong to them. Pain in the blood that I call ink is made within.

www.ingramcontent.com/pod-product-compliance
Lightning Source LLC
Chambersburg PA
CBHW061633130726
47996CB00003B/1263